EXTREME EARTH

50

SCIENCE
EXPERIMENTS
TO MAKE AND DO

SilverDolphin

Silver Dolphin Books

An imprint of Printers Row Publishing Group
A division of Readerlink Distribution Services, LLC
10350 Barnes Canyon Road, Suite 100, San Diego, CA 92121
www.silverdolphinbooks.com

Written by Joe Fullman
Illustrated by Adam Linley, Daniel Sanchez Limon,
Keri Green, and Martyn Cain/Beehive Illustration

Printers Row Publishing Group is a division of
Readerlink Distribution Services, LLC.
Silver Dolphin Books is a registered trademark of
Readerlink Distribution Services, LLC.

All notations of errors or omissions should be addressed to
Silver Dolphin Books, Editorial
Department, at the above address. All other correspondence
(author inquiries, permissions)
concerning the content of this book should be addressed to
Quarto Children's Books Ltd,
The Old Brewery, 6 Blundell Street,
London N7 9BH UK.

ISBN: 978-1-68412-330-8

Manufactured, printed, and assembled
in Shenzhen, China HH/05/18

22 21 20 19 18 1 2 3 4 5

EXTREME EARTH

50

SCIENCE EXPERIMENTS TO MAKE AND DO

JOE FULLMAN

Silver Dolphin

CONTENTS

GET STARTED

Explore Planet Earth with these 50 fun experiments. From mini volcanoes to rain gauges, these easy-to-do projects show how the world works. Find out about the inside of the Earth, rocks and minerals, the atmosphere, and the water cycle. See how magnetism can tell you where you are, and learn how to build your own weather station.

To begin, make your test tube stand by following the instructions on page 7. Then use the items in the tube and pocket, along with everyday objects from around the house, to carry out your scientific investigations.

SAFETY MESSAGE

Some of the steps in these experiments may be dangerous, such as cutting items with knives. Follow the instructions carefully and ask an adult to help you when you see this symbol:

Equipment

Inside the test tube and box, you'll find these items. Look out for this symbol (right)—it will show you which bits of equipment you can use from your kit.

ou will ne
- coffee filter pape
- toothpick
+ test tube
  nonpermane

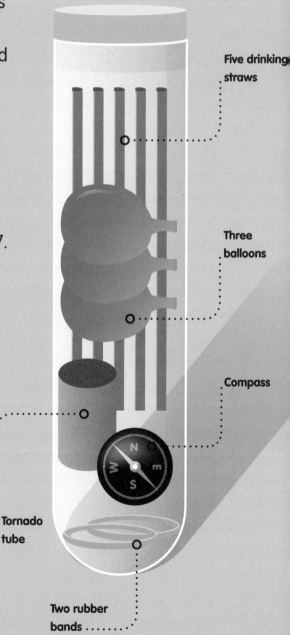

Five drinking straws

Three balloons

Compass

Tornado tube

Two rubber bands

CARD KIT 1

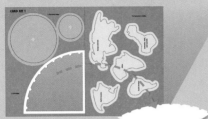

CARD KIT 2

Simply press out the parts you need

CARD KIT 3

CARD KIT 4

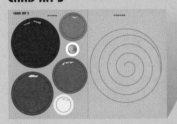

CARD KIT 5

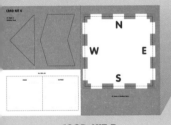

CARD KIT 6

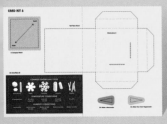

MAKE YOUR TEST TUBE STAND

1 ⚠️   Tab A · · · · · · · · · · ·

Ask an adult to score and fold along all the lines on piece 1 from card kit 6. Fold it into a box shape and glue down Tab A to hold it in place. Glue down the two long tabs for a neat finish.

2 ⚠️

Ask an adult to score and fold along the lines on piece 2 from card kit 7. Fold in the tabs on the small rectangles on piece 1. Push them into the slots on piece 2.

3

Open out the tabs on the small rectangles on piece 1 to hold it in place.

4

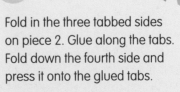

Fold in the three tabbed sides on piece 2. Glue along the tabs. Fold down the fourth side and press it onto the glued tabs.

THE EARTH IN SPACE

The Earth is our home in the Universe. It is one of eight planets—plus countless smaller bodies—that orbit the Sun. Together, all these bodies make up the Solar System. The four planets nearest to the Sun, including Earth, are small and rocky, while the four farthest from the Sun are huge giants made of gas.

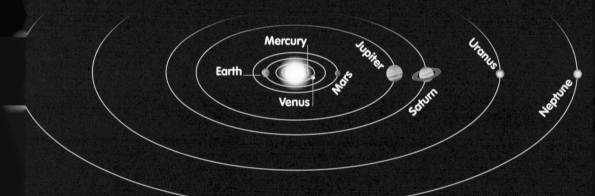

The whole Solar System is held together by **gravity**. This is a force that pulls objects toward each other. The greater an object's **mass**, the stronger its gravity. The Sun is by far the biggest object in the Solar System—making up 99.8 percent of its mass. So it has very strong gravity, which keeps the planets orbiting around it.

The planets spin on their axes as they orbit the Sun. However, none of the planets orbit in a perfect circle. Instead, they all follow a slightly stretched circular path that is known as an ellipse.

ORBITING MASSES

The Earth isn't actually a true sphere. Forces exerted by the Earth's rotation cause it to bulge slightly in the middle. This means that the diameter of our planet is around 26 miles greater measured east to west than it is north to south. Its shape is technically known as an **oblate spheroid**.

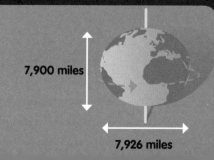

7,900 miles

7,926 miles

1: PLANETARY BULGE

You will need:

+ card circles from card kit 1
- wooden skewer
- modeling clay
- scissors
- paper
- tape

1 Push out the two card shapes and ask an adult to punch out holes in their centers using the skewer. Push the larger circle on the sharp end of the skewer so it's about an inch from the end and hold it in place with some modeling clay.

2 Cut out four paper strips, 12 inches by 1 inch. Tape them together so they form an equal cross shape. Punch a hole in the center of the cross and at the ends of each strip.

3 Put the blunt end of the skewer through the hole in the middle of the cross and slide it down. Curve each of the cross strips up and put the skewer through the holes in the ends. Slide the center of the cross down onto the large circle and stick it in place with tape. Put the smaller card circle on the blunt end of the skewer to keep the paper in place.

Make sure the pieces of paper can move up and down the skewer easily.

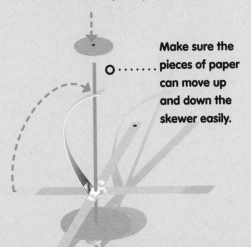

4 Pull the paper so that it's stretched out between the two card circles. Then, holding the skewer by its blunt end, spin it like a top. What happens to the strips of paper?

WHAT'S HAPPENING?

As it spins, the paper should bulge out to become an oblate spheroid, just like Earth. This is because the spinning creates a force that pushes the paper outward and away from the central point around which it is moving.

2: ELLIPTICAL ORBITS

1

Put a large sheet of paper on the corkboard and push the two pushpins into it so they sit about an inch apart in the center of the paper.

2

Cut a piece of string 14 inches long. Knot the ends together to make a small loop about 6 inches long. Place the loop over the pins.

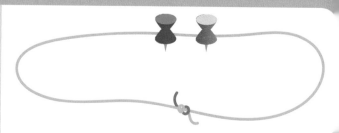

3

Put a pen inside the string and, pulling the string taut, draw a shape all the way around the pins. What shape have you drawn?

WHAT'S HAPPENING?

When the pins are close together, the shape drawn is a slight ellipse. This is just like the orbits of the planets, including the Earth. When the pins are put further apart, the shape is a much longer, thinner ellipse. This represents an object orbiting the Sun much further out, such as a comet.

4

Move the pins so they're about 4 inches apart and repeat the experiment using the other color pen. What shape have you drawn now?

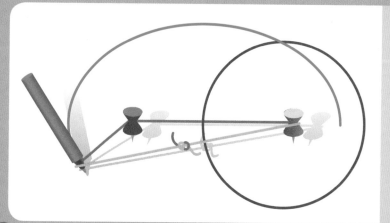

3: ASTROLABE

1

Push the card shape out. Ask an adult to poke a hole through the marked spot using scissors. Ask an adult to cut a 6-inch piece of string and pass one end through the hole and tape it to the back of the card.

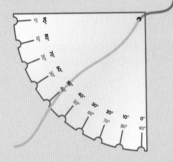

You will need:

- **+** card astrolabe from card kit 1
- scissors
- string
- metal nut or washer
- **+** straw
- tape

2

Tie the washer to the other end of the string. Ask an adult to cut the straw to the right length and attach with tape to the top of the card as shown.

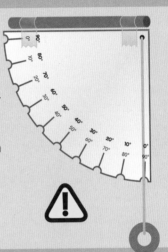

3 On a day when the Sun is visible in the sky, hold the astrolabe straight in front of you with the straw at the top. Angle it toward the Sun so that the sunlight shines through the straw to form a circle of light on your hand. Don't look directly at the Sun. Note the angle marked by the hanging string. Repeat this experiment every hour over the course of a day. Do your measurements change at all?

WHAT'S HAPPENING?

Because Earth is spinning, the Sun appears to move through the sky during the day, rising in the east and setting in the west. As it appears to move, its height in the sky changes. It is low in the sky in the morning and evening and will reach its highest at about midday.

MEASURING AND MAPPING

The most accurate way to represent Earth is as a globe—but a globe isn't very convenient to carry around, so people tend to use flat maps instead. However, representing the curved Earth in a flat form will always cause some areas of the map to look distorted.

Projections

Imagine you could peel the surface of Earth like an orange. If you were then to flatten the peel down, there would be gaps between parts of the world. To make a map, you'd have to fill in the gaps by stretching the areas of land so they joined up. This is known as making a projection.

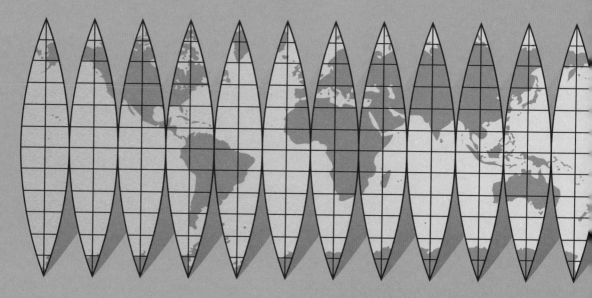

WHERE ARE YOU?

The Earth's metal **core** creates a magnetic field that effectively turns Earth into a giant magnet. You can use a device called a compass to detect this field and guide yourself around. It has a magnetized needle that always points north.

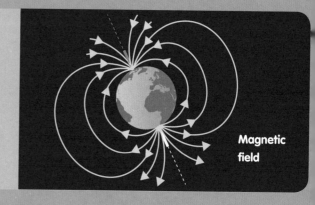

Magnetic field

4: MAKING A COMPASS

You will need:
- steel needle
- bar magnet
- tape
- thin piece of cork or foam
- nonmetallic bowl
- water
- **+** compass

1
Magnetize the needle by stroking it with the magnet. Do this around 50 times, always in the same direction. Use a small piece of tape to attach the needle to the cork.

2
Fill the bowl with water, and carefully place the cork and needle in the middle of the bowl. Does the needle stay still or does it move to point in a particular direction? Compare its movement with the compass from the kit.

WHAT'S HAPPENING?
Rubbing the needle with the magnet turns it into a mini-magnet. All magnets point north. Placing the needle on the water allows it to move freely until it is pointing north.

: COMPASS WATCH

1
You can use a watch (with hour and minute hands) to find out which way is north if you haven't got a compass. First, make sure it's set to the right time. If you are in the northern hemisphere, place your watch on a flat surface and rotate it so that the hour hand is pointing at the Sun.

Sun

You will need:
- watch with hands
- **+** direction card from card kit 6

3
In the southern hemisphere, point the 12 at the Sun. Place the card between this mark and the hour hand to get your north-south line.

2
Push the card shape out of card kit 6 and position the southern end so it's halfway between the hour hand and twelve o'clock. This is your south-north line.

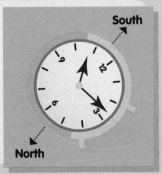

South

North

WHAT'S HAPPENING?
Although the position of the Sun in the sky changes during the year, it is still constant enough for us to be able to find out which way is north.

6: MEASURING MAGNETIC FIELDS

1 Place the magnet so it's sitting horizontally on the paper as shown and trace around it. Take the compass and place it half an inch away from the south end of the magnet.

You will need:

+ compass
• bar magnet

• paper
• pencil

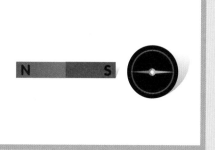

2 Trace a circle around the compass. Note which direction the red needle of the compass is pointing, then remove the compass and draw an arrow in the circle showing the direction the needle was pointing.

3 Move the compass up and to the left about an inch. Then repeat step 2.

4

Keep repeating steps 2 and 3, moving the compass and drawing arrows until you have drawn circles all the way around the magnet. What direction are the arrows pointing?

WHAT'S HAPPENING?

The position of the arrows shows the bar magnet's magnetic field, which is like a miniature version of Earth's magnetic field. Like poles (two north poles or two south poles) repel each other. Unlike poles attract. The compass needle is a mini magnet. Its north pole points toward the bar magnet's south pole and away from its north pole.

INSIDE THE EARTH

When the Earth formed, it was a hot mass of boiling rock on which nothing could survive. Gradually it cooled, forming layers with all the heaviest material sinking to the center, while a solid **crust** formed on the outside.

LAYERS AND LAYERS

The crust, the outer layer of solid rock on which we live, is also by far the thinnest layer—just over 40 miles deep at its thickest point. Below this is a great churning expanse of slowly moving rock, known as the **mantle**, which extends down for 1,800 miles.

At the center of the Earth is a metal core, measuring 4,350 miles across, which is made up of two parts: a liquid outer core and a solid inner core, consisting mainly of iron and nickel. The core is about the size of the planet Mars.

Crust . . . . ○
Mantle . . . . ○
Outer core . . . . ○
Inner core . . . . ○

Brittle crust

Earth's crust isn't completely solid. There are weak points where **lava** (molten rock) erupts out of **volcanoes**. Elsewhere, superheated water is forced out of gaps in the form of **geysers** (on land) and **hydrothermal vents** (on the sea floor). Some scientists believe that life on Earth may have begun in the mineral-rich water around a hydrothermal vent.

7: EARTH BOOK

1 Push the four card shapes out of card kit 2.

You will need:

+ Earth book shapes from card kit 2
• paper fastener
• pens and pencils
• scissors

2

Place the largest circle on the table, then lay the other circles on top in decreasing order of size.

3

Line the cards up so that the labels are sitting on top of each other. Ask an adult to make a small hole in the middle with the scissors.

4 Push the paper fastener through the center of the cards. Split the metal pieces at the back and push flat to secure.

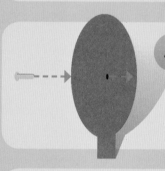

5

On each label, write the name of the layer of Earth it represents: crust, mantle, outer core, inner core, as well as some fascinating facts about each layer.

Crust

Mantle

Outer Core

Inner Core

WHAT'S HAPPENING?

Once you've got the paper fastener in position, you should be able to spin the labels round so you can read the facts about each layer. Although this model gives you an idea of how much of the Earth remains hidden from view, it's not completely accurate. If it were, you wouldn't really be able to see the crust, because it is so thin in comparison to Earth's other layers.

8: TABLETOP VOLCANO

You will need:

- tray
- modeling clay
- baking soda
- liquid soap
- food coloring
- vinegar

1 This experiment is going to get messy, so make sure you gather all your equipment onto a tray first—and ideally do it outside.

2

Use a 6-inch ball of modeling clay to make a mountain shape in the middle of the tray. Push your fingers into the top of the mountain to form a **crater**, turning the mountain into a volcano. The crater should almost—but not quite—reach the bottom.

3

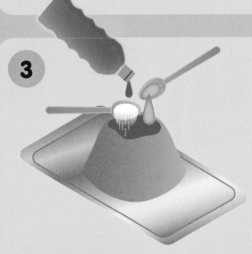

Carefully tip a tablespoon of baking soda into the crater. Then add a tablespoon (0.5 fl oz) of soap and a few drops of food coloring.

4 Add ¼ cup (2 fl oz) of vinegar to the crater and stand back.

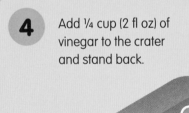

WHAT'S HAPPENING?

The vinegar and baking soda react to make a gas called **carbon dioxide**, which produces lots of bubbles. This causes the mixture in the crater to foam up and pour out the top of the crater. In a volcano, the bubbles form as the lava rises up through the crust.

9: MODEL GEYSER

You will need:

- large bottle of diet soda (the bigger the better!)
- + test tube
- salt

1 This experiment makes a big mess, so make sure you do it outdoors and use diet soda so things don't get too sticky.

2 Place the soda bottle on the ground and carefully open the lid.

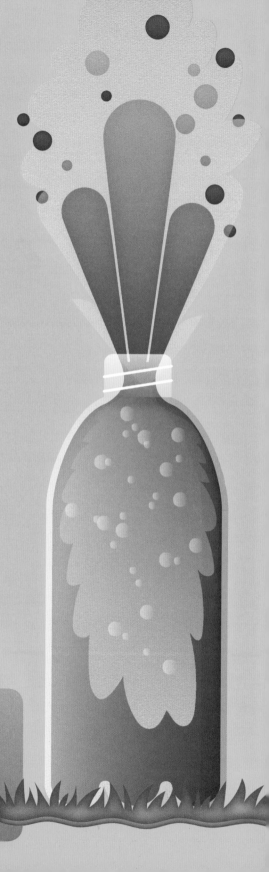

3 Fill the test tube with salt. Quickly, pour the salt into the top of the soda bottle in a single motion.

4 Run away! Quickly!

WHAT'S HAPPENING?

Soda is made fizzy by being pumped full of carbon dioxide. Usually the gas comes out of the drink by forming bubbles at a steady rate. However, the rough surface of the salt granules causes thousands of bubbles to suddenly form on them all at once. The released gas pushes the liquid out of the top of the bottle in a rush, causing a soda geyser.

10: HYDROTHERMAL VENT

1

Fill the bowl with cold water and place it on a flat surface, such as a table.

2

Use the scissors to cut a piece of string about 20 inches long. Tie the middle section of the string around the neck of the small bottle, leaving the two long ends free.

3

Pour a few drops of food coloring into the small bottle, then get an adult to help you fill it almost to the brim with hot water.

4

Using the strings as handles, carefully lower the small bottle into the bowl of cold water so it rests on the bottom. What happens to the colored water inside the glass bottle?

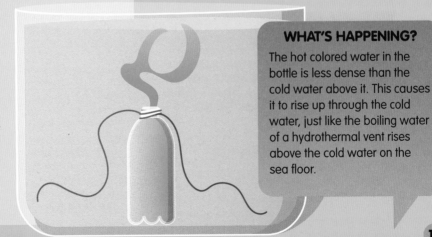

WHAT'S HAPPENING?

The hot colored water in the bottle is less dense than the cold water above it. This causes it to rise up through the cold water, just like the boiling water of a hydrothermal vent rises above the cold water on the sea floor.

GIANT JIGSAW

Earth's crust is divided into a number of pieces, known as **tectonic plates**, which fit together like a giant rock jigsaw. The plates are very slowly—but continuously—moving, as they are pushed around by currents in the mantle.

Around 270 million years ago, all the continents were joined together in a giant landmass called **Pangaea**. Over millions of years, the movement of tectonic plates broke Pangaea up, creating the continents we have today. Powerful forces are at work along the boundaries where tectonic plates meet. Rocks are pushed up to form mountain ranges or pulled down to melt and form powerful volcanoes. Earthquakes happen where two or more plates meet.

Earth's plates were once joined as Pangaea.

11: EARTHQUAKE TABLE

1 Ask an adult to cut two pieces of cardboard from your pizza box, around an inch bigger than your baseplate on all sides. Stack up the baseplate and cardboard pieces and attach them together using two rubber bands, one at either side, around two inches from the end.

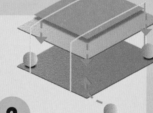

2 Insert the rubber balls between the two pieces of cardboard, one in each corner.

You will need:

- pizza box (or thick cardboard)
- + two large rubber bands
- building bricks
- building bricks baseplate (about 10 inch x 10 inch)
- four small rubber balls
- scissors

3 Make a tower using the building bricks, two blocks wide and 20 blocks high. Then pull the baseplate horizontally a couple of inches and let it go. What happens? Try building your tower twice as wide and half as tall. What happens now?

WHAT'S HAPPENING?

In an earthquake, most of the damage is caused not by the ground going up and down, but when it moves from side to side. This experiment shows how the taller and thinner the structure, the more damaging these forces can be.

12: TECTONICS IN ACTION

1

Push the card shapes out. Note how some of the pieces, such as South America and Africa, seem to fit together like a jigsaw, showing that they were once joined.

You will need:

+ **five continents from card kit 1**
- foam
- foil tray or baking pan
- measuring cup
- tea light
- books
- water

2 Trace the shapes of the continents onto a piece of foam, then cut the pieces out.

3 On a heat-resistant surface, place two books of roughly the same size about a foot apart and put the tray on top of them so there's a space under the center of the tray. Half fill the tray with water.

4 Carefully place your foam continents on the water in the center of the tray, so there's a gap in the middle of them. Ask an adult to light a tea light and place it directly under the gap between the foam continents. Does anything happen to the continents?

WHAT'S HAPPENING?

As the water at the bottom of the tray heats up, it becomes less dense and so rises above the cooler water above it. But as it reaches the surface, it cools and sinks again. This causes a circular motion, moving the foam continents on the water's surface apart. Known as a **convection current**, this is a model of what happens in the Earth's mantle—on a much bigger scale and over a greater time period— to move the continents of the crust.

13: EARTHQUAKE WAVE BOX

1

Ask an adult to cut the lid off the cardboard box, using the scissors. Then get them to make two small holes in opposite ends of the box, as shown.

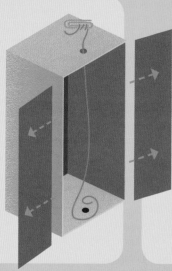

2

Cut a piece of string so that it's a couple of inches longer than the box. Tie one end onto a paper clip and thread the other end through a hole at one end of the box.

3

Pull the string through, so it's being held at one end by the paper clip. Then pass the loose end through the hole at the bottom of the box. Pull it tight, and tie it to another paper clip to keep it in place.

4

Attach the four other paper clips to the vertical string. Place the box on a table and then bang the table hard with your hand. Do the paper clips move?

WHAT'S HAPPENING?

When an earthquake strikes, it sends shock waves traveling through Earth. These can cause buildings to sway or even fall down. Hitting your hand on the table has a similar effect. It causes a shock wave that passes through the table to the box, making the string wobble (the paper clips help you to see this clearly).

ROCKS AND MINERALS

All rocks are made up of a mixture of elements (which are made up of just one type of atom) and minerals (which are compounds of two or more elements found in rocks). There are three main types of rock, which are categorized according to how they are formed: **igneous**, **sedimentary**, and **metamorphic**.

ROCK TYPES

Igneous rock forms when molten rock (**magma**) is forced up through Earth's crust and slowly cools to become solid. Igneous rocks are usually quite hard.

Sedimentary rock is formed when small pieces of rock or organic matter are laid down as **sediment** and then compressed together. All **fossils** form in sedimentary rock.

Metamorphic rock forms when rocks are subjected to extreme heat and/or **pressure**, which changes their character.

Sedimentary rock

The rock cycle

Rocks don't stay the same type forever. All rocks are worn down by wind and rain to form sediments, which can be squeezed underground to form sedimentary rocks. Rocks can be buried by earth movements, and heated and squeezed to form metamorphic rocks. If rocks are heated even more, they may melt. This molten rock then solidifies to form igneous rocks. This constant movement from state to state is known as the rock cycle.

14: ROCK IN A CUP

1

Pour the gravel, sand, and soil into one of the plastic cups. Completely cover them with water. Use the stirrer to mix them all together. Then leave them for a day.

You will need:

- two see-through plastic cups
- gravel
- sand
- soil
- water
- stirrer
- sugar
- teaspoon
- scissors

2

After a day, the particles should have settled into layers in size order with the largest at the bottom and the smallest at the top. Carefully pour away as much water as you can.

3

In a separate cup, make a **solution** of one cup of water and five teaspoons of sugar. Stir the sugar until it has all dissolved, then pour the mixture onto the layers in the other cup so that they are moist, but not soaking wet. Leave them to dry.

4

When dry (this may take a few days), ask an adult to cut away the plastic cup. What has happened to the layers of gravel, sand, and soil?

WHAT'S HAPPENING?

Particles mixed together will settle in size order. The largest and heaviest particles will settle first and form a layer at the bottom and the smallest and lightest will form a layer at the top. In order to become hard rock, the grains must become welded together by minerals in the water— just as these particles have been stuck together by the sugar.

15: SEDIMENTARY BREAD

1 Trim the crusts from six slices of brown bread, then do the same with six slices of white bread. Stack the slices in a pile, alternating white and brown slices. Use the ruler to measure the height of the stack.

You will need:
- white sliced bread
- brown sliced bread
- ruler
- two sheets of waxed paper
- four heavy books

2 Place the bread stack on a sheet of waxed paper, then place the other sheet on top. Balance the books on top of that. Leave your pile undisturbed for about a week.

3 Remove the books and measure the pile with the ruler. How does it compare to the height of the pile at the start? What do the layers look like?

WHAT'S HAPPENING?
The bread layers should now be squashed together. This is what happens to the layers of sedimentary rock on the sea floor as more and more sediment is deposited on top of them.

16: DINOSAUR TRACKS

1 Mix two cups of flour, one cup of salt, and one cup of water in the bowl. Add a few drops of food coloring. Knead the dough for at least five minutes until it has a smooth consistency.

2 Roll the dough out until it's about an inch thick. Then, wet one hand and press it into the dough with your fingers spread out. Leave the dough to air dry for a couple of days.

You will need:
- measuring cup
- flour, 2 cups
- salt, 1 cup
- water
- mixing bowl
- food coloring
- rolling pin

WHAT'S HAPPENING?
As the dough hardens, it keeps the imprint of your hand. Millions of years ago, a dinosaur walking in soft mud might leave behind a footprint. If the mud hardened, it could turn into a type of fossil known as a trace fossil or imprint fossil, like the imprint of your hand.

17: LANDSLIDE!

You will need:

- eight identical coins
- two paper towels
- stiff cardboard
- scissors
- tape

1 Place two piles of two coins side by side. Cut off a piece of tape that's long enough to wrap around both piles of coins.

2 Place the two piles side by side in the center of the tape (on the sticky side) and then stick the ends of the tape together over the top of the coins to make a coin packet.

3 Repeat steps 1 and 2 with the other four coins. Cut out a piece of paper towel that's the same width as the coin packet and long enough to wrap around it. Wrap it around the coin packet and stick it to the top with tape.

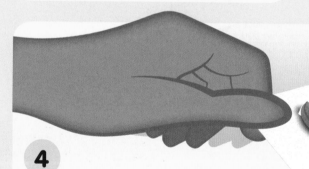

4

Lay a second piece of paper towel onto your stiff cardboard and stick it in place with tape. Place both coin packets onto one end of the towel. Then gently lift the side of the card where the coins are sitting into the air until one of the packets slips. Which one goes first?

WHAT'S HAPPENING?

Landslides occur when the force of gravity pulling objects downward overcomes the force holding them on a slope. In nature, this can be caused by many factors, including earthquakes, storms, and soil **erosion**. In this experiment, the coin packet in a paper towel has more friction against the slope than the smoother packet, helping it to resist moving down the slope for longer.

18: STALACTITES AND STALAGMITES

1 Place the jars on the tray about 6 inches apart. Ask an adult to fill the jars with hot water, almost to the top. Then stir in a few drops of food coloring. Add tablespoonfuls of Epsom salts until no more can be dissolved.

2 Cut a piece of string long enough to reach the base of each jar with a little bit left over. Attach a paper clip to either end of the string.

3 Drop the ends of the string into the jars. The string should dip slightly between the two jars. What happens after a few days?

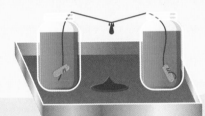

You will need:
- two jars
- tray
- hot water
- food coloring
- Epsom salts (magnesium sulfate)
- two paper clips
- tablespoon
- string

WHAT'S HAPPENING?
As the water drips down and **evaporates**, the minerals solidify forming **stalactites** (from the string down) and **stalagmites** (from the tray up).

19: QUICKSAND

1 Pour a cup of cornstarch into your mixing bowl. Slowly mix in half a cup of water with your fingers until you have a gloopy mixture. Gently push your fingers into the mixture, then try to pull them out suddenly. What happens?

2 Slowly stir your fingers through the mixture, then try stirring quickly. Is it easier or harder? Lift up a handful of the mixture and let it drip out. Then try slapping the mixture. Does the mixture's texture change?

You will need:
- cornstarch
- water
- liquid measuring cup
- mixing bowl

WHAT'S HAPPENING?
Just like quicksand, this mixture behaves differently depending on pressure. When it's handled gently, the grains in the cornstarch flow past each other and act like a liquid. But when it's hit quickly, the grains lock together and it acts like a solid.

20: CANDY ROCK CYCLE

1 Take four candies of different colors and ask an adult to cut them into small pieces using scissors. Mix the pieces up, then use your hands to mold them into a ball. Sedimentary rocks are formed in this way.

You will need:
- chewy candy
- scissors
- see-through plastic bag
- heavy book
- heavy-duty aluminum foil

2 Put the candy rocks into the plastic bag. Warm it between your hands until it's pliable and then squeeze. Take the book and press it down on the candy. Metamorphic rocks are formed in this way.

3 Line a nonstick pan with several layers of foil. Take the candy out of the bag and place it in the pan. Ask an adult to heat the pan on a stove until the candy completely melts.

4 Ask an adult to take the saucepan off the heat. Leave the candy to cool and harden. Igneous rocks are formed in this way.

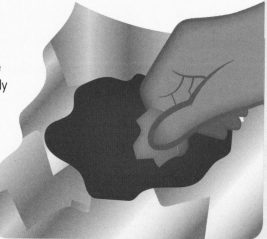

WHAT'S HAPPENING?
This experiment replicates with candy what happens during the rock cycle. First the small candy pieces are squashed together like sedimentary rock. Then, they're changed by heat and pressure like metamorphic rock. Finally, they're made molten and left to harden, like igneous rock.

A WORLD OF WATER

Earth is dominated by water, which covers 71 percent of the planet's surface. Here it exists in all three of its states: liquid, solid, and gas. Liquid water forms the oceans, rivers, and underground reservoirs called aquifers. Solid water makes up the polar ice caps and glaciers, while water in its gas state, known as vapor, is in the atmosphere.

THE WATER CYCLE

Water is constantly moving between the surface and the atmosphere in a process known as the water cycle. The Sun's heat evaporates water from the surface of seas and oceans. It rises into the air where it forms clouds, which may be carried over land by winds. Water falls to the ground as rain (or snow), before draining back into the ocean.

Weathering

Water can be destructive, but it can also create new landscapes. On land, rocks are broken up by the weather in a process known as **weathering**. Streams and rivers then carry away these tiny pieces of rock in a process known as erosion. These tiny pieces of rock (sediment) are carried down to the sea by rivers, where it settles and hardens to form sedimentary rocks.

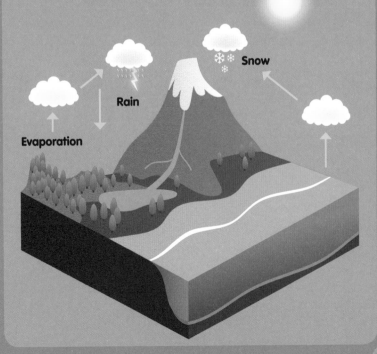

Snow

Rain

Evaporation

21: WATER CYCLE IN A BAG

You will need:

- **+ test tube**
- **+ plastic straw**
- see-through ziplock plastic bag
- strong tape
- food coloring
- water

1 Fill the test tube with water almost to the brim. Add four drops of blue food coloring and use a straw to stir it in. Pour it into the bag.

2 Zip the bag shut and tape it to a window that gets plenty of sunlight. Leave it for five days and watch what happens to the water? Does it just stay at the bottom of the bag?

WHAT'S HAPPENING?

If the Sun is shining, you should be able to observe a mini water cycle, as the water in the bag evaporates into vapor, **condens** into mist, and then drips back down the sides as precipitation.

22: CLOUD IN A BOTTLE

You will need:

- see-through plastic bottle with a twist-off cap
- water
- teaspoon
- matches

1 Put a teaspoon of water in the bottle. Ask an adult to light a match, drop it in the bottle and then quickly screw the cap back on.

2 Squeeze the bottle several times. What happens?

WHAT'S HAPPENING?

When the lid is screwed on the bottle, the match should go out, leaving smoke particles around which water droplets form, creating a cloud. Squeezing the bottle raise the temperature of the air, turning the water back into vapor so it seems to disappear. Expanding the bottle again causes the temperature to reduce and the cloud to reform.

23: RIVER EROSION

You will need:

- foil tray or oven dish
- soil or potting compost
- plastic cup
- scissors
- liquid measuring cup

1

Half fill your tray with soil. Then rearrange the soil into a slope, so it's higher on one side than the other. On the shallow side, clear the soil to leave a one-inch gap at the end of the tray. This will be your "sea."

2

Ask an adult to make a small hole in the bottom of the plastic cup with the scissors.

3

Hold the cup over the top of the soil slope and carefully pour water into the cup so that it comes out the bottom in a single, flowing line.

4

Keep pouring until all the water has gone. Where does it end up? What does it do to the soil?

WHAT'S HAPPENING?

The water flows downhill taking the path of least resistance. As it flows, it washes away material—in this case, soil. The water that collects at the bottom should contain pieces of soil that have been eroded from the slope.

24: GLACIER MOVEMENT

1

Mix a cup of cornstarch with a quarter of a cup of water until you get a substance with the rough consistency of toothpaste.

You will need:

- cornstarch
- water
- dry and liquid measuring cups
- bowl
- spoon
- map printout of a country or continent
- sand

2 Place a golf ball size lump of the mixture on your map. Watch what happens. Is the mixture moving?

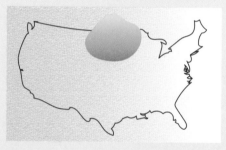

3 Put another lump (about half as big as the first) on top of the mixture in the middle.

4 Sprinkle a little sand around the edge of the mixture. What does the mixture do to the sand?

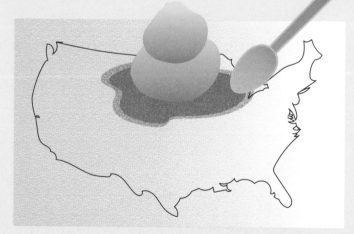

WHAT'S HAPPENING?

Glaciers may look like giant solid lumps of ice, but they're actually moving very slowly. During very cold periods, known as ice ages, they can take over large areas of land, just like your mixture is doing. The second smaller blob represents fresh snowfall, pushing down on the glacier and making it spread out further. As they move, glaciers pick up boulders and carry them vast distances, just as the mixture is doing with the grains of sand.

25: SINKING AND FLOATING

1

Fill the test tube with water from the faucet and place it in the test tube holder.

2

Pick a small grape (small enough to fit inside the test tube) and drop it into the water. The grape should sink to the bottom.

You will need:
- + test tube
- grapes
- salt
- tablespoon

3

Tip the water and grape out and refill the test tube with water. Add tablespoons of salt, stirring it until no more dissolves.

4

Now drop the grape back in the test tube. Does it behave differently this time?

WHAT'S HAPPENING?

When the grape is dropped into fresh water from the tap, it sinks because it's denser than the water. Adding salt increases the water's mass but without increasing its volume by very much, so it also increases its density. Once the water is really salty, it will be denser than the grape, and the grape will float. The saltiness and temperature of seawater affects its density and can affect how ships and icebergs float in it.

WATER OF LIFE

Water also makes up around 60 percent of you. It is the most important substance on Earth. Without it, no life could exist.

People need fresh water to survive, but most of the water on Earth is salty seawater. More than 96.5 percent of all the water is in the salty oceans. Of the remaining fresh water, 1.75 percent is locked up in ice caps, glaciers, and permanent snow, leaving the rest to be shared across the world. But, of course, fresh water is not distributed evenly. Some places receive so little water that droughts are common.

Roots draw water up from the ground

The oceans cover about 71 percent of Earth's surface . . . .

People have discovered how to clean and desalinate (take the salt out of) water to make it safe to drink. Like plants with long root systems, they can source water deep underground by digging wells. People can grow crops in areas that receive little rainfall by using a process called **irrigation**. This involves digging channels to divert water from rivers and streams into fields.

26: CUP IRRIGATION

1 Ask an adult to make one hole on each side of the first cup just up from the bottom. In two other cups, make a hole near the top on one side and near the bottom on the other. In the last two cups, make a hole in one side near the top.

You will need:
- five plastic cups
- scissors
- + two plastic straws
- modeling clay
- books
- water

2 Cut the straws in half and attach them to the cup holes, using the books to arrange the cups as shown. Use modeling clay to make the joins watertight. Then, slowly pour water into the first cup and watch what happens.

WHAT'S HAPPENING?

Most traditional irrigation systems rely on gravity, like this, drawing water from a high reservoir to low fields. Here, the water flows down through the straws and into the lower cups.

27: CLEAN WATER

1

Half fill the bowl with water. Mix in three tablespoons of salt and also put in a handful of soil, so that the water is both salty and dirty.

You will need:

- large bowl
- water
- tablespoon
- salt
- soil
- spoon
- small cup or glass
- plastic wrap
- **+ large rubber band**
- small rock

2

Place the cup in the center of the bowl. Its top should be shorter than the bowl but higher than the water.

3

Cut a piece of plastic wrap a few inches bigger than the bowl on all sides. Place it loosely over the bowl and use a rubber band to attach the plastic to the outside of the bowl.

4

Place a stone in the center of the plastic so it pushes the plastic down. You want as big a slope as possible. Leave your contraption outside in the sunshine for a day and then check it to see what's happened.

WHAT'S HAPPENING?

Clean water should have collected in the cup. When the water in the bowl is heated by the Sun, it evaporates into a gas, leaving the salt and soil behind. When the gas hits the plastic, it condenses again into droplets, which roll down the underside of the plastic into the cup.

28: WALKING WATER

You will need:

- seven plastic cups
- liquid measuring cup
- spoon
- food coloring (red, yellow, and blue)
- paper towels
- water
- tray

1 Line the seven cups up in a row on the tray and label them 1, 2, 3, 4, 5, 6, and 7.

1. 2. 3. 4. 5. 6. 7.

2 Take the liquid measuring cup and pour water into cups 1 and 7, so they're half full. Pour the water into cups 3 and 5 so they're three quarters full. Cups 2, 4, and 6 should remain empty.

1. 2. 3. 4. 5. 6. 7.

3 Put a few drops of red food coloring in cups 1 and 7 and stir. Then put yellow food coloring in cup 3, and blue food coloring in cup 5, and stir.

1. 2. 3. 4. 5. 6. 7.

4 Take a paper towel and fold it into a strip, then hang it between cups 1 and 2, so one end is in the water, touching the bottom of cup 1 and the other is touching the dry bottom of cup 2. Do the same between the other pairs of cups as shown. Leave for a couple of hours.

WHAT'S HAPPENING?

The water should have transferred between the cups, mixing the colors together in cups 2, 4, and 6. The water has been drawn up the paper towels by a process called capillary action, which is also how plants draw water from the ground.

1. 2. 3. 4. 5. 6. 7.

EARTH'S ATMOSPHERE

Above the sea and land, Earth is surrounded by a thin blanket of gases called the atmosphere. This protects us from the Sun's harmful rays during the day, and retains the Sun's heat at night, helping to keep the planet warm.

The layers

The atmosphere can be divided into layers. The air is thickest near the planet's surface, and gets thinner as the altitude increases.

- **Troposphere** (0–7 miles): The lowest layer is where we live and where most of the weather takes place.
- **Stratosphere** (7–30 miles): The calm layer above the weather, this contains the ozone layer which screens the Sun's dangerous UV rays.
- **Mesosphere** (30–50 miles): This is where tiny rocks from space usually burn up as shooting stars as they head toward Earth.
- **Thermosphere** (50–440 miles): Charged particles from space collide with atoms in this layer to produce the colorful displays known as the **aurora borealis**.
- **Exosphere** (440–6,000 miles): The outermost layer is where the atmosphere finally fades away into space.

Earth

Troposphere

Stratosphere

Mesosphere

Thermosphere

Exosphere

ATMOSPHERIC AIR

Nitrogen

Water vapor and other gases

Oxygen

By far the most common gas in the atmosphere is nitrogen, which makes up over three quarters of the total. Oxygen, which is vital to many life forms—including us—makes up around 20 percent. The rest is composed of small amounts of water vapor and other gases, including carbon dioxide (0.04 percent).

29: UP AND UP

1 Push the card shapes out of card kit 3. Ask an adult to make a hole in each circle's center, using the scissors. Place the largest card down flat. Then place the other cards on top of it from biggest to smallest with the centers lined up.

2 Push the paper fastener through the center of the cards. Split the metal pieces at the back and push flat to secure.

You will need:

+ atmosphere circles from card kit 3
• paper fastener
• scissors

WHAT'S HAPPENING?

Once you've got the paper fastener in position, you can see the layers of the atmosphere surrounding Earth like a giant gas blanket. The Troposphere, the lowest level, is by far the thinnest layer—and yet, without it, life on Earth couldn't exist.

30: THE WEIGHT OF AIR

1 Blow the balloons up so they're the same size. Close them by tying string around their openings, then use the string to tie the balloons to either end of the ruler.

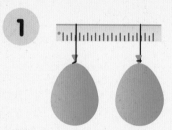

You will need:

+ two balloons
• string
• ruler

2 Tie another length of string halfway between the balloons, so the balloons will hang at the same height. Then untie one balloon and let half the air out. Reattach it to the ruler. Does it still balance?

WHAT'S HAPPENING?

Air has mass and weight. When you blow into the balloon, you're increasing its density because the air inside is at greater pressure than the air outside. When both balloons are the same size, they balance. As soon as you let air out of one, the other will sink because it contains more air and weighs more.

Half fill the large container with water. Turn on the flashlight and hold it against the side of the container pointing at the water. You shouldn't be able to see a beam of light.

Add ¼ of a cup of milk to the container and stir it in. Hold the flashlight up to the side again. You should now be able to see a faint beam of light.

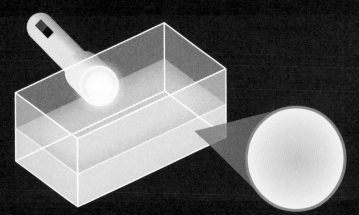

Add a full cup of milk and stir it in. Hold the flashlight up again. Look at the beam from the other side of the tank. What does the light look like now?

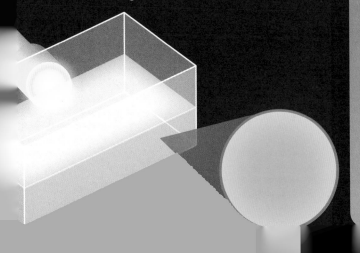

WHAT'S HAPPENING?

The particles of milk in the water scatter the light, just as particles in the atmosphere do. Blue light is scattered most, which is why the beam near the flashlight and the daytime sky (when sunlight has the shortest distance to travel) look blue. At sunset and sunrise, sunlight has to travel through more air to reach us, by which time the blue light has been scattered. Adding the milk has the same effect: the red, orange, and yellow colors are scattered least, so the light appears orange.

WHAT IS WEATHER?

The weather is the current atmospheric conditions: how hot or cold it is, whether it's dry or rainy, windy or still, and whether the skies are clear or overcast. The weather in an area can change day by day but, over time, a pattern will emerge. This long-term pattern is known as the **climate**. Weather is fueled by the energy of the Sun and, in particular, the variations in heat that it produces across the globe.

Sunlight

Sunlight is much more intense around the center of the Earth, near the Equator, than it is to the far north and south, which is why it's hot in the tropics and cold in polar regions.

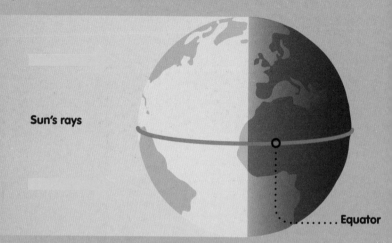

Sun's rays

Equator

Winds

The Sun's heat warms air near the Equator and this warm air rises and spreads north and south where it cools and sinks, creating winds. The rotation of the Earth also affects winds, causing them to spiral, which can cause hurricanes and cyclones.

Precipitation

The Sun's heat also causes water to evaporate into the air as vapor. When it cools and condenses, it falls back to Earth as precipitation, usually either as rain in warm areas or snow in cold ones.

Seasons

Over a year, Earth completes a single orbit of the Sun. Because Earth is tilted, different parts of the planet are pointing at the Sun at different times of year. These differences cause the seasons.

Fall

Summer

Winter

Spring

You will need:

- white wall or a large piece of white paper
- glass jar
- flashlight
- tape
- liquid measuring cup
- small mirror
- water

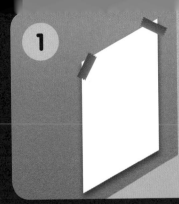

1 Stick the white paper to a wall or use a white wall if you have one.

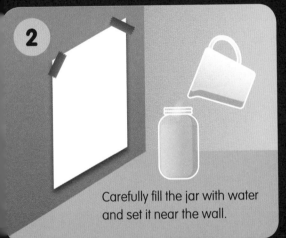

2 Carefully fill the jar with water and set it near the wall.

3 Place the mirror inside the jar and tilt it so it's at an angle, pointing toward the wall.

4 Turn out the lights so it's dark (you may also need to draw the curtains) and shine the flashlight into the jar at the mirror. Look at

WHAT'S HAPPENING?

If the mirror is tilted correctly (it may need some adjusting), you should see a rainbow on the paper or wall. This is because the light hitting the mirror is being bent, or refracted, by the water. This causes the light to be split into its seven constituent colors: red, orange, yellow, green, blue, indigo, and violet. This is also what happens in nature when light is bent by water droplets to form a rainbow.

33: SNOWFLAKE ID

1 When it starts snowing, push out the snowflake chart from card kit 6.

COMMON SNOWFLAKE TYPES

Simple Prisms	Plates	Dendrites	Columns	Needles

TEMPERATURE CONDITIONS

All temperatures	25 to 32°F, below 15°F	25 to 32°F, -7 to 15°F	15 to 25°F, below -7°F	15 to 25°F

HUMIDITY CONDITIONS

Low humidity	Low to medium humidity	Medium to high humidity	Medium humidity	Medium humidity

You will need:

+ snowflake ID chart from card kit 6
- black paper
- small stones
- magnifying glass

2 First, you need to cool the paper down so snowflakes will land on it without melting. Put it outside somewhere dry, cold, and covered for around 20 minutes.

3 Once the card is cold enough, put it out in the snow so flakes can fall on it. Weigh it down with stones.

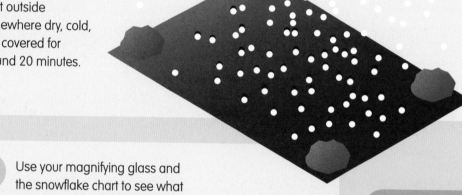

4 Use your magnifying glass and the snowflake chart to see what sort of flakes you have. You'll have to look quickly before the flakes melt.

WHAT'S HAPPENING?

Snowflakes form when a water droplet freezes around a speck of dust in the sky. As the water freezes, its molecules form a six-sided shape: a hexagon. As more water vapor freezes onto the crystal, they add to its shape. Each flake forms in a unique way, which is why no two snowflakes are alike. However, certain types do tend to form in certain temperatures—as the chart shows.

4: WHAT IS WIND?

1

Push out the spiral shape from card kit 3. Carefully pull the spiral apart.

2

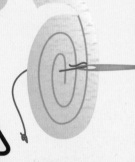

Tie a knot in the end of the thread. Thread the other end of the thread onto your needle and get an adult to push it through the center of the spiral shape.

3 Tie the other end of the thread to the skewer and make sure that the card spiral can spin freely.

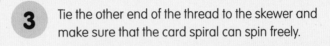

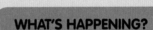

WHAT'S HAPPENING?

Hot air is less dense than cold air. The hot air above the lamp rises, causing the spiral shape to spin. On a much larger scale, hot air near the surface of the Earth rises up through the colder air above it. But as it gets higher, it cools, so it sinks again. It's this constant rising and falling of air that creates wind.

4

Turn on the table lamp and dangle the spiral directly over the bulb. Be careful not to touch the bulb. As the light warms up, what happens to the spiral?

35: TORNADO TUBE

You will need:

- two 1-liter plastic bottles
- water
- **+** tornado tube

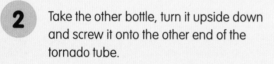

1 Fill one bottle with water up to about the ¾ mark. Then take the tornado tube and screw it on to the neck of the bottle.

2 Take the other bottle, turn it upside down and screw it onto the other end of the tornado tube.

3 Carefully turn the bottles over. To begin with, the water should stay in the top bottle, held there by the pressure of the air below it.

4 Spin the two bottles around a few times. What happens now? Next time try adding some food coloring and soap to the water for added color and bubbles.

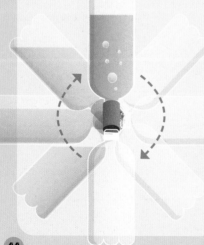

WHAT'S HAPPENING?

Spinning the bottles starts off a tornado effect and the air and water in the bottles to spin with them. The air spins around and goes up into the top bottle, while water spins around it as it goes down to the bottom bottle.

MEASURE THE WEATHER

We have various ways of measuring the weather. At a local level, weather stations are packed with devices for measuring things like temperature, rainfall, and wind speed. High above our heads, satellites keep track of large-scale weather fronts. All this information helps us to predict both what the weather, and the overall climate, will be like in the future.

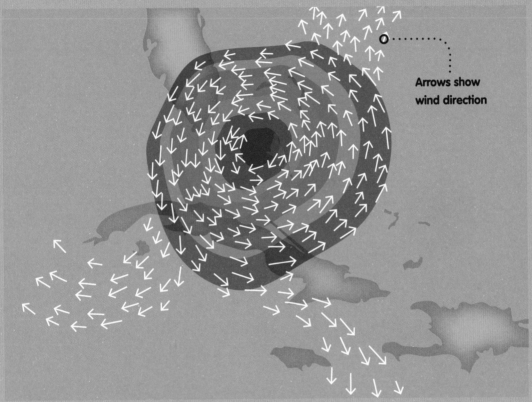

Arrows show wind direction

Weather map showing a hurricane in the Caribbean

The most commonly used weather-measuring devices are:

Rain gauge
For measuring the amount of rain that has fallen in a specific time period.

Thermometer
For measuring the air temperature.

Wind vane
For measuring the direction of the wind.

Barometer
For measuring air pressure.

Anemometer
For measuring wind speed.

Hygrometer
For measuring how humid the air is.

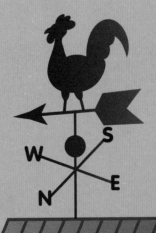

36: MAKE A THERMOMETER

You will need:

- 1-liter plastic bottle
- food coloring
- water
- + plastic straw
- modeling clay
- felt-tip pen
- bowl
- ice

1 Squeeze a few drops of food coloring into the bottle. Then fill the bottle up to the brim with room-temperature water.

2 Push the straw 2 inches into the bottle and put modeling clay around the rim to keep it in place. The water will have risen up the straw slightly. Mark its new position with your pen. This is your base level.

3 Ask an adult to boil some water. Half fill the bowl with the hot water. Carefully place your bottle thermometer in the bowl. Once it's settled, mark where the water level is in the straw. Is it above or below the previous mark?

4 Take the bottle out of the bowl and ask an adult to empty the hot water. Pack ice around the bottle until the bowl is full. Look at where the water level is in the straw. Is it above or below the previous mark?

WHAT'S HAPPENING?

As water heats up, it expands and should rise in your straw. When it gets cold, the opposite should happen. Traditional thermometers measure temperatures using rising and falling liquids like this.

37: MAKE A WEATHER VANE

1 Put the piece from card kit 4 with the compass points marked on it flat on a table. Place a piece of modeling clay in the middle of the card. Stick the pointed end of the pencil in the clay so it's sticking up. Line the card up to north using the compass.

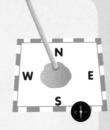

You will need:

+ card pieces from card kit 4
• pencil with eraser on the end
+ compass
+ plastic straw
• modeling clay
• scissors
• pin

2 Ask an adult to cut ½-inch notches at either end of the straw. Slot the card pointer in one end and the tail in the other. Push a pin through the center of the straw and into the eraser. Make sure the straw can spin freely. Now take it outside and see what happens when the wind catches it.

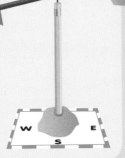

WHAT'S HAPPENING?

The wind pushes the arrow around so that it points in the direction the wind is coming from. Being able to tell wind direction helps weather forecasting, as a sudden change in the wind's direction usually means that bad weather is on its way.

38: MAKE A RAIN GAUGE

You will need:

+ test tube
+ test tube stand
• tape
• ruler
• marker pen
• funnel
• clear plastic bag
+ rubber band

1

Cut some tape that's the same length as the test tube. Using the ruler and marker, mark measurements along the tape. Then stick the tape to the test tube and put it in the stand.

2 Put the plastic bag around the test tube and stand and secure it in place with the rubber band. Put the funnel in the top and then leave your gauge outside. See how much rain collects in the test tube and record the measurement each day.

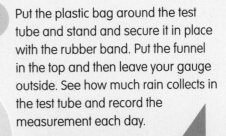

WHAT'S HAPPENING?

As any rain falls, it collects in the funnel and runs into the test tube.

39: MAKE A BAROMETER

1

Cut the neck off the balloon. Attach the rest over your jar and pull it down so it fits tightly and is stretched tight over the jar's opening. Secure it with the rubber band.

You will need:
+ balloon
• glass jar
+ rubber band
+ plastic straw
• tape
+ card pointer from card kit 6
+ test tube stand
• paper
• pen

2

Stick the straw to the top of the jar, so its end is in the middle of the balloon. Press out the card pointer from card kit 6 and stick it to the other end of the straw. This is your pointer.

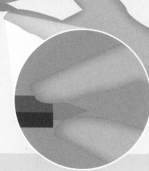

3

Stick a small piece of white paper to the back of the test tube stand. Put your barometer in front of it and mark the position the pointer points to. Record the pointer's position every time there's a change in the weather. What do you notice?

WHAT'S HAPPENING?

If your pointer is higher, it should be fine weather, but if it's lower, it should be poor weather. This is because high pressure—which presses down on the balloon, and raises the pointer—is caused by descending air, which is dry because it has come from the upper atmosphere. It warms as it descends, so any water in it is not going to condense and form clouds. Areas of low pressure are caused by rising air, which cools as it rises and the water in it condenses to form clouds.

40: MAKE AN ANEMOMETER

1 Ask an adult to push the skewers through one of the paper cups, just below the rim, to form a cross. Ask an adult to cut out a small square of cardboard and tape it to the underside of the crossed skewers, as shown.

2 Ask an adult to push each of the other cups onto the ends of the skewers. The skewers should be an inch below the rims, as shown. Use some tape to hold them in place.

3

Turn your device over and ask an adult to punch a hole in the bottom of the center cup using the sharp end of the pencil. Push the pencil, eraser first, into the cup so the eraser is resting against the cardboard. Turn your device back over and ask an adult to push the pin down through the cardboard and into the eraser.

Be sure to get the pin as close to where the skewers cross as possible . . . .

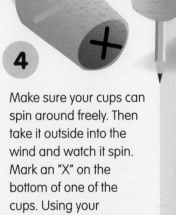

4 Make sure your cups can spin around freely. Then take it outside into the wind and watch it spin. Mark an "X" on the bottom of one of the cups. Using your stopwatch, count how many times the device spins all the way around in a 30-second period.

WHAT'S HAPPENING?

An anemometer is a device for measuring wind speed. A stronger wind will blow the anemometer around more times in the 30 seconds.

41: MAKE YOUR OWN HYGROMETER

1 Firmly glue the straw to one of the scales near the top of the cone. Press out the pointer from card kit 6 and stick it to the end of the straw to be your pointer.

2 Stick some white paper to a vertical surface, such as a window. Put your hygrometer in front of it and mark the position of the pointer. Continue marking the pointer's position every day for a week.

You will need:
+ card pointer from card kit 6
• an open pine cone
• glue
+ plastic straw
• tape
• piece of paper

WHAT'S HAPPENING?

Your hygrometer should give you a rough idea of how humid the air is. When the air is humid, the pine cone contracts to protect its seeds, raising the pointer. But when the air is dry, the pine cone opens up to release its seeds, lowering the pointer. The higher the pointer, the more humid it is.

42: MAKE A WEATHER STATION

1

Gather all your weather-measuring devices together. Put your barometer and hygrometer on a windowsill next to a blank piece of paper. Outside, stand your weather vane and anemometer upright using large pieces of modeling clay and put your thermometer and rain gauge next to them.

You will need:
• your thermometer
• your weather vane
• your barometer
• your anemometer
• your hygrometer
• your rain gauge
• modeling clay
• pens and paper

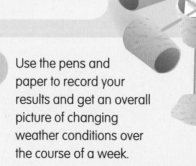

2 Use the pens and paper to record your results and get an overall picture of changing weather conditions over the course of a week.

LIFE ON EARTH

The Earth is the only place in the entire Solar System where life is known to exist. From basic beginnings 3.8 billion years ago as simple single-celled organisms, life has evolved into an amazing variety of life forms today.

 Archaea

 Bacteria

 Protists

Fungi

Plants

 Animals

Six kingdoms

Scientists categorize all life into six groups known as kingdoms. Three of these six groups—archaea, bacteria, and protists—are single-cell organisms. The other three are complex life forms: fungi, plants, and animals. In total, more than 2 million species have been identified on Earth, but there may be millions more to discover.

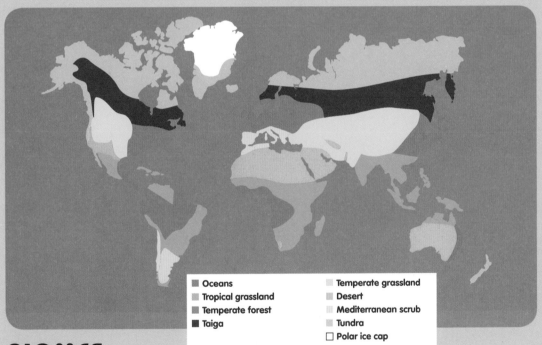

- ◼ Oceans
- ◼ Tropical grassland
- ◼ Temperate forest
- ◼ Taiga
- ◻ Temperate grassland
- ◻ Desert
- ◻ Mediterranean scrub
- ◻ Tundra
- ◻ Polar ice cap

BIOMES

Life exists almost anywhere on Earth where there is water and nutrients. Life forms have been found thriving in some extremely inhospitable places, including frozen Arctic waters and even around vents spewing out superheated water on the ocean floor. Different species form communities called ecosystems. Large ecosystems are known as biomes.

43: BACKYARD BIODIVERSITY

You will need:

- plastic container with lid
- hole punch
- **+ two plastic straws**
- nylon stocking or pantyhose
- tape
- plastic wrap
- magnifying glass
- scissors
- string

⚠️

1

Punch two holes in the container on either side, just under the rim. Insert the end of a straw into one of the holes. If it's loose, use tape to hold it in place.

2

Cut a piece of nylon stocking about 6 inches square. Tape it to the other straw so that the gauze of the stocking is covering one end. Then push the covered end of the straw through the other hole in the container.

3

Ask an adult to cut out the plastic center of the lid, leaving just the rim. ⚠️ Stretch a piece of plastic wrap across the container and hold it in place by putting the lid back on and snapping it in place.

4

Go to an area where insects are common, such as your backyard, and mark out an area 3 feet by 3 feet using string. Now hunt for insects. When you see a small one, put the end of the non-covered straw next to it and suck hard through the covered straw. If you've made your device correctly, the insect should be sucked into the container—and not into your mouth!

WHAT'S HAPPENING?

This is a good way of testing biodiversity: how many living things there are in a particular area of habitat. Try testing different areas, such as a lawn, woodland, or next to a pond. What area has the greatest amount of insect life?

44: BOTTLE BIOME

1

Ask an adult to cut the bottle in half. Put the top half to one side and put about an inch of gravel in the bottom half. Fill up the rest of the bottom half, almost to the top, with potting soil.

You will need:

- large plastic bottle
- scissors
- gravel
- potting soil
- water
- moss
- clear tape
- measuring cup

2

Moisten the soil all the way through and then plant your mosses. You can use several different species.

3

Ask an adult to make four small downward cuts at the top of the bottom section of the bottle. Squeeze the side together with one hand and slide the top half of the bottle over the bottom half by about an inch. Secure with tape.

4

Place your bottle somewhere that receives a lot of light.

WHAT'S HAPPENING?

Your bottle now encloses a complete ecosystem that should have everything it needs. Tiny microorganisms and insects in the soil produce carbon dioxide. Plants use this, along with sunlight and water, to photosynthesize, producing oxygen, which is then used by the organisms. Water evaporates from the soil in the day, collecting on the inside of the bottle before dropping back down into the soil to restart the process.

45: BLUBBER GLOVE

1

Fill the bowl about half full with cold water and ice cubes. Dip your hand in the water. It's pretty cold, right?

You will need:

- large bowl
- water
- ice
- two ziplock freezer bags
- shortening
- tablespoon
+ rubber band

2

Put four tablespoons of shortening into one of the ziplock bags. Put the rubber band around your wrist. Put your hand in the empty bag and then put this in the bag with the shortening. Use the rubber band to keep both bags on your hand (and to stop the shortening from getting out).

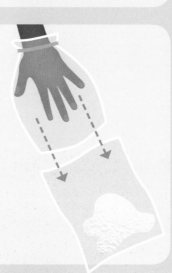

3

Spread the shortening around the bag so that it covers the inner bag covering your hand.

4

Put your hand back in the water? What does the temperature feel like now?

WHAT'S HAPPENING?

The thick, fatty shortening acts like the layer of fat or blubber on Arctic animals, such as whales and walruses. This layer keeps the heat in and the cold out—just like the shortening in the glove is doing.

FRAGILE PLANET

Scientists believe that the world is warming up, which may have serious consequences for the future of life on Earth.

In the past 200 years, the burning of **fossil fuels**, such as coal and oil, has increased the amount of carbon dioxide in the atmosphere, making it retain more heat. In this period, global temperatures have risen by an average of 1.8°F. That may not sound like a lot, but it's caused large areas of sea ice to melt in the Arctic. If the climate changes and temperatures continue to rise, more ice will melt, raising sea levels around the world and flooding coastal areas.

The Greenhouse Effect

Without the atmosphere it would be too cold for life to exist on Earth. Gases such as carbon dioxide, methane, and water vapor let the Sun's heat through to the planet, but also prevent it from escaping back into space—just like the panes of glass in a greenhouse do, which is why they're also known as greenhouse gases. However, if the amount of these gases increases, they will retain more heat, which could potentially raise temperatures to dangerous levels. This is known as the greenhouse effect.

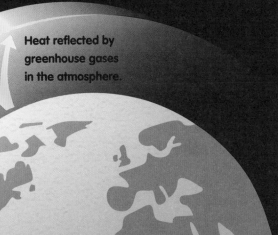

Heat reflected by greenhouse gases in the atmosphere.

46: DIRTY AIR

You will need:

+ card pieces from card kit 4
- petroleum jelly
- magnifying glass
- small stones

1 Push out the card pieces from the kit. Smear some petroleum jelly in the middle of both cards to cover an area about 2 inches square.

2 Place the card marked "inside" on a flat surface inside your house where it won't be disturbed, such as a windowsill.

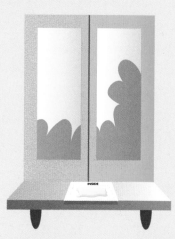

3 Place the other card outside on a flat surface, such as a table. Put it somewhere where it won't be disturbed, and ideally at a time when no rain is forecast for the next few days. Weigh it down using small stones on its corners.

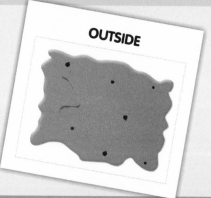

4 Leave both cards in place for a week. Then gather and compare. Do they look different? If you look at them closely through the magnifying glass, what can you see?

WHAT'S HAPPENING?

The petroleum jelly will catch any particles in the air. The inside card will probably have some dust and hairs on it, but it will probably look much cleaner than the outside card, which may be covered in soil, pollen, and exhaust particles from cars. Outside air is generally more polluted than inside air.

47: ACID RAIN

You will need:
- three plastic cups
- vinegar
- water
- chalkboard chalk

Water

Half and half

Vinegar

1 Fill one of the cups with water. Fill the second cup with an equal mixture of water and vinegar. Fill the third cup with vinegar.

2 Put a piece of chalk into each of the cups. Leave for 24 hours.

Water

Half and half

Vinegar

3 Take the pieces of chalk out of the cups. Do they look different from before? Do they look different from each other?

Water

Half and half

Vinegar

WHAT'S HAPPENING?

The smoke and fumes from coal-burning power stations and other factories can mix with water vapor in the air to create a harmful, acidic mixture called "acid rain." When it falls, it can damage the stone of buildings, much like the acidic vinegar has done to the chalk. The more acidic a liquid is, the more damage it causes, which is why the chalk in the pure vinegar has changed the most.

48: MELTING POLES

1

Build a "continent" of modeling clay in the middle of your container, just shorter than the height of the container. It can be any shape but make sure it doesn't touch the sides. Flatten the top.

You will need:

- modeling clay
- see-through plastic container
- permanent marker
- ice cubes

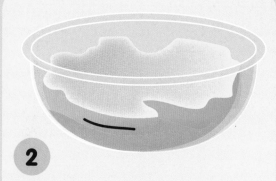

2

Pour water into the container until it's about a third of the way up your continent. When it's settled, mark the level of the water on the outside of the container with your marker.

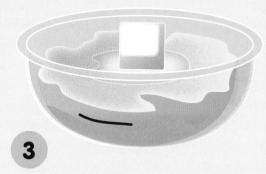

3

Place several ice cubes onto your continent. Press them into the clay so they're secure. Then put your container somewhere warm and allow the ice to melt.

4 On the side of your container, mark the new level of the water. Is it higher or lower than the previous level?

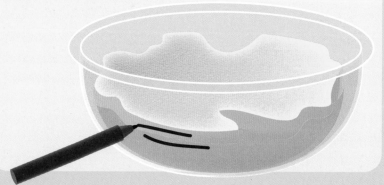

WHAT'S HAPPENING?

Your clay and ice cubes represent Antarctica, which is a large continent completely covered in a thick layer of ice. Scientists believe that if the ice melts because of global warming it will raise sea levels—just like the water level in your container rose. This could flood many low-lying parts of the world.

SUSTAINABLE LIVING

We are going to have to change the ways in which we generate power if we are going to prevent global warming from getting any worse. This will mean moving away from burning fossil fuels to relying on more sustainable forms of energy.

In order to secure a healthy future for the planet, we will have to reduce levels of air pollution. The burning of fossil fuels, both to produce electricity and to power vehicles such as cars and planes, releases thousands of harmful particles into the air. In built-up areas, polluted air sometimes forms thick clouds called smog, which can cause severe breathing difficulties for the people living there.

New technologies

The problem with fossil fuels is not just that they give out pollution and raise temperatures, but that there's only a certain amount of them. One day, they'll run out, and we need to make sure that we've discovered other energy sources by then. Many experts believe that we should focus on developing renewable energy sources such as solar power, wind power, and wave power.

Wind turbine

Solar panels

49: SOLAR OVEN

1 Draw a square on top of your pizza box, 1 inch from the edge on all sides. Ask an adult to cut out three sides to make a large flap.

2 Cover the underside of the flap with aluminum foil. Make sure it's flat and smooth, and use tape to secure it.

3 Cover the hole in the lid you cut in step 1 with clear plastic wrap and stick in place with the tape. Make sure the plastic wrap forms an airtight seal.

4 Cover the inside of the pizza box with foil. Then cover the base with a square of black paper, cut to size.

WHAT'S HAPPENING?

The sunlight is reflected by the foil into the box where the black paper helps to absorb the light and heat. Temperatures can reach 160°F (perhaps even hotter on a sunny day), which is hot enough to warm (if not cook) food.

5 On a hot day, put a slice of cold (cooked) pizza inside the box and place it in direct sunlight. Adjust the flap so it's reflecting sunlight directly onto the pizza. You can use the straw to balance the lid. Leave for 30–45 minutes.

0: WATERWHEEL

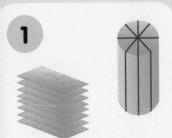

1

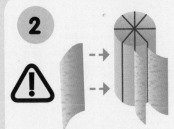

Push out the shapes from card kit 5. Turn the cork on its end and, using the ruler and pen, draw four crossing lines to divide the top into eight equal segments. Continue the eight lines down the length of the cork.

2

Ask an adult to use the craft knife to make slots along each of the eight lines around $\frac{1}{8}$ inch deep. Push the card shapes lengthwise into the slots and curve them slightly, so they're all pointing in one direction.

You will need:
+ card shapes from card kit 5
- cork
- ruler
- pen
- craft knife
- large plastic bottle
- wooden skewer

3

Ask an adult to cut off the top of the bottle around 3½ inches from the top. Then cut a scoop out of one side of the bottle, around 3 inches wide and 1½ inches deep. Ask an adult to poke holes either side of the bottle.

4

Ask an adult to cut a skewer in half. Poke each half through the holes in the bottle and into the ends of the cork. Check that the cork can spin freely.

WHAT'S HAPPENING?
The water should turn the paddles, which spins the cork, turning the skewer. In olden times, waterwheels were used to power machinery in mills and factories. They're very environmentally friendly machines as they use a renewable form of energy: flowing water.

5

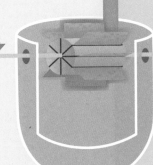

Now place your construction under the faucet so that the water hits the cardboard paddles.

GLOSSARY

AURORA BOREALIS
Colored lights that form high in the atmosphere and are caused by the interaction between charged particles from the Sun and particles in the atmosphere.

CARBON DIOXIDE
A colorless and odorless gas that is found in the atmosphere and is released by living organisms during a process called respiration.

CLIMATE
The weather conditions that a location experiences over a period of time.

CONDENSE
When a gas cools to form a liquid.

CONVECTION CURRENT
The circular movement of a liquid or gas caused by warm matter rising, then cooling and spreading out, falling again, then being heated once more.

CORE
The very center of something. Earth's core is divided into two parts, the inner core and outer core.

CRATER
A large hole. In the case of a volcano, the crater is the vent through which liquid lava pours out.

CRUST
The outer layer of something. Earth's crust is a very thin layer of rock that sits on top of the mantle.

EROSION
The wearing down and removal of rock. This process can be carried out by moving water, such as waves or rivers, or the wind.

EVAPORATE
When a liquid turns into a gas.

EXOSPHERE
The outermost layer of Earth's atmosphere which merges into space.

FOSSIL
The hardened remains of an ancient animal or plant that is found inside rocks.

FOSSIL FUELS
Fuels that are made from the fossilized remains of plants and animals. They include coal, oil, and natural gas.

GEYSER
A hole in the Earth's surface out of which super hot water and steam burst, sometimes in towering jets.

GRAVITY
An attractive force produced by objects that have mass. The more mass an object has, the greater its gravitational force. So a massive object, such as a star, will have stronger gravity than a less massive moon.

HYDROTHERMAL VENT
A crack in the Earth's surface that is underwater and through which super hot water gushes. This water is usually rich in minerals that support colonies of deep-sea creatures.

IGNEOUS
A type of rock that is formed when liquid rock cools and solidifies.

IRRIGATION
A system of pipes and channels that carries water to plants.

LAVA
The name given to liquid rock that has broken out onto the Earth's surface.

MAGMA
The name given to liquid rock that is beneath the Earth's surface.

MANTLE
The name given to the thick layer of rock that sits below the crust and above the core.

MASS
The amount of physical matter there is in a substance.

MESOSPHERE
The layer of Earth's atmosphere that sits between the stratosphere and the thermosphere.

METAMORPHIC
A type of rock that has changed its structure because of high levels of pressure and/or temperature.

OBLATE SPHEROID
A shape that resembles a squashed ball.

PANGAEA
The name given to the huge ancient supercontinent that started to break up about 200 million years ago.

PRESSURE
A force created when one object pushes on another.

SEDIMENT
The name given to small pieces of rock that are carried by rivers.

SEDIMENTARY
A type of rock that is formed from tiny particles of sediment that have been squeezed together to produce solid rock.

SOLUTION
A type of mixture where a solid substance, known as a solute, has dissolved into a liquid, known as a solvent.

STALACTITES
A long, thin piece of rock that hangs from the roof of a cave and is formed by slowly dripping water that leaves behind minerals.

STALAGMITES
A long, thin piece of rock that sticks up from the floor of a cave and is formed by slowly dripping water that leaves behind minerals.

STRATOSPHERE
The layer of Earth's atmosphere that sits above the troposphere.

TECTONIC PLATES
The huge pieces of rock that make up the Earth's crust. These plates are pushed around by currents in the molten rock beneath.

THERMOSPHERE
The layer of Earth's atmosphere that sits between the mesosphere and the exosphere.

TROPOSPHERE
The lowest layer of Earth's atmosphere, where the gases are thickest and most of our weather happens.

VOLCANO
A mountain built by lava forced up from beneath the Earth's surface.

WEATHERING
The breaking down of rocks that is caused by the action of water, wind, heat, cold, and even animals and plants.

INDEX